I Went Looking for You

Ruth Lepson

BlazeVOX [books]
Buffalo, New York

I Went Looking for You by Ruth Lepson

First Edition

ISBN: 1-934289-81-7
ISBN 13: 978-1-934289-81-5
Library of Congress Number: 2008940554

BlazeVOX [books]
14 Tremaine Ave
Kenmore, NY 14217

publisher of weird little books

BlazeVOX [books]

blazevox.org

2   4   6   8   0   9   7   5   3   1

DEDICATIONS

To my good friend Celia Gilbert, who gets to the essence of things as well as the specifics, and who painted the portrait of me on the back cover.

To keen-eyed Joel Sloman, who gave me the go-ahead.

To the members of my poetry groups, who sat patiently through my revisions of many of these poems.

To my first love Roy Stevens, who painted the work on the cover.

To smart guys Daniel Bromberg, Luke Moldof, and Joe Moffett, who helped me organize this book.

IN MEMORY OF PATRICIA ZANDER,
who taught all who knew her

ACKNOWLEDGMENTS

With thanks to these publications, in which some of the poems in this book have previously appeared:

AGNI REVIEW—*For the Dead*

CARVE—*Saturation*

COLD MOUNTAIN—*Dissolution*

DJINNI—*Swampscott in a Warm December*

GARGOYLE—*February*

IN THE WEST OF IRELAND (ANTHOLOGY)—*Grasses*

LISTENLIGHT.COM—*Rose*

NAHANT BAY—*Ocean at Bay*

NIGHT HOUSE ANTHOLOGY (Four Zoas Night House Ltd.)—*An Edge of Gold*

NORTHWOODS PRESS ANTHOLOGY—*Dear Winter*

NOON: A JOURNAL OF SHORT POEMS—*Function Theory*

POETRY FROM SOJOURNER: A FEMINIST ANTHOLOGY —*October 7, 1994*
—*They Were*

RIO: A JOURNAL OF THE ARTS—*Swampscott Hour*

RUBY—*Concert at the Gardner Museum*

SOJOURNER—*Anne Sexton on the Cover*
—*October 7, 1994*
—*They Were*

SPECTRUM —*For Georgi Belev*
— *Profile of a Potato Head*

STICKMAN REVIEW—*Lights Across the Bay*

THE LARCOM REVIEW—*This Winter*

THE MID-AMERICA POETRY REVIEW—*Where Seagulls Fly*

THE SOW'S EAR—*Parts of You*

THE WANDERING HERMIT REVIEW—*For Robert Creeley*

THE WOMEN'S REVIEW OF BOOKS —*Breezes*
                                  —*Red Roses*

WORD OF MOUTH, VOL. II—*Lobby of a New York Residential Hotel*

YEFIEF —*Motion Sickness: Pre-occupation*

5__TROPE—*When I Was in Paris* (a section of *Saturation*)

The Poem of J received an honorable mention in the 2001 National Writer's Union Poetry Contest, judged by Philip Levine.

Lobby of a New York Residential Hotel was a semi-finalist in Lamia Ink's Annual International One-page Play Competition.

Saturation was set to electronic music by composer Jean-Francois Claude and performed by him and flutist Mario Caroli at Harvard University, May, 2008.

low road, a jazz & poetry performance group of Noah Preminger on saxophone, Eric Lane on keyboard, and me, has presented some of these poems with settings by Noah & Eric, and a CD is forthcoming.

These Trees is sampled in a composition by Eric Lane entitled 'South End' and played by the hip-hop band Cracker Supreme and by low road.

Table of Contents

I Went Looking for You

THESE TREES

after I've left
these trees
their insistent green humming
will shine
and all my emotions
will have been
just that
mine

SATURATION

rain percussion
frank & detailed discussion
rain freefall
down the long lawn
trees akimbo
house finch nest unblemished

*

it's a sparkling noisemaker Morse code, the sea –
diffuse, and its diffusion
arrives as beauty

words as waves
a flock of words
now it's raining little *t*'s and *o*'s

when fog moves out, fireflies –
sparkles that detach from waves

fir tree fractal glows

frayed elm leaves limbs foreground
a self-contained Chinese brush painting

lines approach sand
endlessly rivulets, fog shifts and
sparkles a distant city
fireworks' insistent sizzle

lines and white dots
on the whole back of the sea

if only I had great wings,
more pleasure;
always preparation and hope

*

lawn, filled with leafy thoughts,
barely notices the small silver plane
emergency vehicles
their urgent sounds
who was hit by lightning

*

egg casings
eyeglasses
shadow of his glasses
crowd sounds
splash

*

trees tuck themselves in at the lake's edge

later, turquoise ring around the moon
neon chartreuse trees wave bizarrely in wind

*

she said
a little cloud fell on her head

*

he was like a tear, clear,
cleansing, visible, quiet

*

cement birdbath capped with 2 feet of snow –
mammoth mushroom

*

when I was in Paris
walking through a prison of rain
rain, not itself unless ceaseless

we walked around the pond in winter

I appreciated what you said
it did no good

swimming in the lake of the poem
a containable longing; later,
longing, again

*

crow nestled in crotch of branches
black in the rain

*

lines of poetry raining down

*

sky again
smashing the windows

*

in the plane I relax when I see
cloud bolsters

*

breezes discombobulate trees
the sea, its seaweed

semaphore clouds

*

I thought it was a bird
it was a leaf
thought it was the phone
it was the shower's overtones
I thought it was you
it was you

*

thin strip of land across the bay
matte finish of the cloudy sky

coral-tinted sky and
the essentials, endlessly fascinating, catch my eye

*

stayed in bed, veiled ocean
then
silver seersucker sea punctuated with sea grass
and this bedroom the seam of the world

*

foam at the ocean's edge spills
over another bunch of foam, beads spilling
over the edge of a dish

*

our antecedent a fishy creature, five-eyed
amuse, from *to stare stupidly*

*

on the window rain as small white cartoonish marks
clumps of leaves behind
consistency of tone essential

*

vertical lines in the digits of my fingers
shelves of books in my library

my immigrant mother's voice, to me accentless, all my life *the* voice

*

peeling bark of the sycamore jigsaw puzzle,
rain pulls the pieces apart

*

light-headed I'm dew-filled,
am able

BREEZES

Spiders shuttle in the winds,
warm ones, and cool.

The oaks across the street are serious
against the young sky.

Dotted gold butterfly
flits among sunflowers,
a flirt among colors unwinding in the breeze.

In the garden,
red, orange and pink, startled.

WHERE SEAGULLS FLY

It's good to walk the dog
when he finally meets
the black cat down the street.
Years, each tiny lesson.

The way seagulls seem to fly at times
against the wind and into the clouds.
It's a white day, white and gray.

It's good to live where seagulls fly,
thick clouds over the gray house.
Spring wind, first night on the porch,
dandelions white,
close to the end of something.

RAIN

Neck arched,
a pigeon stands on the grass,
starlet in a purple-black coat,
nonchalant at the premiere.

Raindrops, miniature tapdancers,
click on the black-flecked road.

Usually I arrive in sun.
Now thunderstruck
the pond puts on a show.

A man with a green cap on and I
watch from box seats in our cars.

Through the tree trunks the band of white lake.
Watch trees and lake turn into a backdrop —

Extras jog, or bike.

An acquaintance said, *Rain makes things clear,*
and it does, so clear they're impossibly three-dimensional.

Down the road, a black truck
curves around the rotary and onto another brilliant street.

OCEAN AT BAY, SWAMPSCOTT

Water like mercury,
blue ice, glint-white, brown,
rolls, fizzes over bricks the car tracks made in grey sand.

Rocks the necks of turtles.
Masts bobbing like pogo sticks.

Two layers of shadows,
one moving stiffly over the other,
like a loom.

A Dalmatian chases pigeons and gives up.
I go into white wooden stores any time I want.
I love this town.

Across the bay the jagged Boston skyline, like me, definitely there,
but so far away it doesn't matter.

SWAMPSCOTT IN A WARM DECEMBER

Ocean's a huge brain:
light thoughts, gray thoughts, trillions
arriving, veering off –
none the truth.

I look up from *Buckshee*
by Ford Madox Ford – there,
running out of the water
a decade earlier – my golden retriever.

How should I treat my mother?
Like a piece of glass,
God says silently.

And I ask
the reason I'm here:
the pleasure of space.
Like a pancake, spreading
across a pan, the sea sizzles at its edge.

SWAMPSCOTT HOUR

Seagulls spread out in a line by the water's edge,
a string of lights unraveling.
Ducks, dark as darkest rocks, form a circle in the sea.

On the drive home, sun huge,
its reflection white gold on telephone wires –
something turning into something new.

Cool wind –
something old.
Black birds fly.
Black stars in a white sky.

LIGHTS ACROSS THE BAY

Natural not to talk of music
while men are working in the sun.
        Rosmarie Waldrop, *Rhapsody*

nearly silent morning
mourning doves rest on branches
sparrows lift

Christmas trim in the tropical garden
through the leaded glass

clouds move on
from this Moorish palace

            *

taking pictures obsessively
finally nauseated by that as by commodities, stopped
saw   :
sky   moon and palm

        the stucco houses half-lit like memories

            *

can't get a handle   on what's real

that's part of why
I like him –
like even his shadow on stucco –

            *

when windows are open –
smooth wind, noise

clear hills
my eyes can feel

＊

why the lights across the bay tremble, nights

＊

yesterday's flurry of snow's today's headline

next to many a color, the tiny surprise of ice

＊

dreamt *he curved our words into colors*
parts of the neon sweep across the San Francisco night

IT

it turns out these feelings
really had nothing to do with you
they go and come
I miss you only in the way
I miss a stain –

it's about the same   amount of pain
still there are variations on the theme
I've grown   but my heart and brain
have fixtures that remain the same
I make my life with the things I can name

TIME LINE

Ragged line,
not from any dream.

Yet dreams magnify sections –
which nearly catch fire.
I wake up,
they shrink back into the line.

And when the line is calmed,
edges fall, into curves,
turning almost over,
times of rest.

FUNCTION THEORY

To the left of zero
and into the center
of negative numbers
to imaginary ones
where beauty
doesn't imply exclusion.
The square root
of a negative
number, thought
forms of a little girl.

RED TREE

When she hugged
she held on,
the thin, mean one.
Then how could you not love everyone? –
even those who wrecked your life,
spoiled every joy.
You want them most –
at least in your imagination.
It's a red tree, life.

REUNION DREAM

At the pool by my house
we stand close to each other.
Between the women and men there's less difference.
All gentle, all willing to swim.

Transparent waves,
sun.
We dive
into green water, thin again.

But over my shoulder,
standing by the edge,
some people – I've known them recently –
won't jump in.

I'm turning and floating.
My body tells me things.
But something in me says
the water's amorphous, deceptive,
I can't leave behind anyone who loves me.

FOR THE DEAD

Coming back from vacation, I passed a cemetery with a sign that read *Pray for Us*. I had thought that, if anything, *they* were praying for *us*. Now the black, hollow notes of Shostakovich, September and the oval leaves of the locust, matter-of-fact, push me to work.

Maybe in Purgatory a woman waits for us to lift the shadow that falls on her, the shadow we can still move in this changeable place. Maybe all we can do for the dead is give up our poses, since after life there is no more silence over a meadow, there are no sparrows, whose explosion into the sky sends a ripple through our patient bodies.

THIS WINTER

Driving towards the sunset –
navy, peach, and white – I look
at the guy in the next car
chewing bread contentedly,
wind and snow –
people lonely on earth together –
the chubby baby boy in the cart
at the checkout counter delighted
when I waved from my own place in line.

Two feet of snow
accumulate slowly through the week –
I shovel till my back says
take a break – the way I gardened
each day in July.

Winter clothes for my aging parents,
showed them retirement homes, it's finally ok
they won't know me, just
wanting them to be happy.

It's movement that's beautiful,
movement of the discarded Christmas tree
across the street, tinsel
shimmers in wind –
movement and stillness,
these days, home in
snow.

Microorganisms
living under rocks
at the ocean bottom –
chemosynthesis,
a newfound way of loving.

RED ROSES

The room is so quiet I hear the air, blur of traffic.
The deep green of the ivy in the planter settles me,
the high-intensity lamp yellows the table legs.
Radiators decorate the apartment like silver bracelets.
Tonight, with a quiet wildness, the roses open.
Red is the color, Mother, natural to me.

PRAYER

thin little man
made in Shakespeare's time
in another country   stands
with a stick, or walks,
I can't tell   why
of all the tiles in Amsterdam
I picked this one –
maybe he's
my own dear father, blind,
lying like an egg afraid to crack,
in a bed, his 24-hour house,
maybe this man, who makes a shadow
and wears a tall and tilted hat
is still, content

MOTET FOR MOM

"What would you like for Mother's Day?"

"Did you hear the word 'nothing'?"

"I wish I could wave a magic wand and make you feel better."

"You are magic. When you're here it's magic."

"You say such sweet things."

"I say such sweet things because I have sweet thoughts."

"I don't like your blouse."

"My darling daughter."

"Do you think about Dad a lot?"

"Not a little and not a lot."

"Do you like the video about the history of the Jews?"

"It's not a question of liking it or not liking it."

"I'll do whatever you think I should."

"Do you like it a lot when I come to visit?"

"It's not out of this world."

"Why not?"

"It's in the world."

"Are you thinking a lot about your life?"

"Um hum."

"You're such a devoted daughter....

"When you get a lot of food it makes you happy."

"Want to keep reading Henry Moore?"

"That's enough. It's not so interesting. You can take it away."

"The television has the word 'Lifetime' on it.

"I'm tired. I don't feel like sleeping.

"It looks ridiculous to call this picture 'Lifetime.'

"Go home soon. It's enough."

"I don't feel good now.

"No, I don't want any more.

"I won't say anything, I'll just rest."

"Who's that?"

"That's somebody on TV, Mom."

"There must be a thousand people here."

"We're in the emergency room, Mom, and it's crowded."

"Chippy Cookie....I shall depart and go home."

"This Henry Moore sculpture doesn't impress me....

"What's so funny?"

"Do you believe in God, Mom?"

"A little."

"Do you like the snow, Mom?"

"Yes, I like the snow. Do you?"

"Yes."

"It's a white world. Enjoy the day. What are you coughing for?"

"I have a cold. It's nothing, Mom."

"It doesn't have to be something."

"I became a mathematician when I started thinking about mathematics."

"How old are your boys, Franca?"

"3 and 6"

"Bring the 6-year-old."

"Do you love me because I'm your mother or because I'm lovable?"

"I could eat chocolate all day long....

"Actually, it's not true. You cannot eat chocolate all day long."

"I'm lucky I opened my eyes....

"You could never come to visit enough....

"This chocolate cake is heavenly.

"It's good for us both to see each other, especially if there's also chocolate involved."

"Whatever you have in your house is yours."

"Mom, what are you thinking about?"

"You ask too much of a person."

"Mom, what are you thinking about lately?"

"Set theory."

"Mom, what're you thinking about these days?"

"I'm thinking about my past and about your past."

"Mom, what are you thinking about?"

"The weather."

"What do you think about?"

"Everything that happens at that moment."

THE POEM OF J
after Harold Bloom and David Rosenberg's *The Book of J*

I asked A about it. He laughed and said I already knew about it, still, he didn't seem to realize my problems were with me.

I asked B about it and she was very upset and said my life was hard and her life was hard.

I asked C about it and her answer was very interesting and well put but I couldn't apply it to me.

So I asked D about it and he spent many years giving me the answer, little by little, but at this rate I'll never get it.

I asked E about it and he made some disparaging remark and wanted to talk about money.

I asked F about it. She didn't want to talk about it.

I asked G about it and we had a very intense conversation, after which he disappeared and never came back.

I asked H about it but there was a question of confidence that got in the way, over and over again.

So I called I about it since of all the people I know he seems to know most about it, but by the time I reached him I was tired and couldn't sustain the conversation.

Finally I talked to J about it, who is dying this year, and who didn't feel very much in his life and invented a persona more consciously than most of us do and he said he hoped he'd find feeling and learn to love and learn to die.

I wished him luck and he was astonished that I was crying, since we had been out of contact for years but now all that had angered me seemed petty.

OCTOBER 7, 1994
 for Sally Sedgwick

The shadows of the bicycles are sharp
on the yellowing brick path,
yellow mums under the lamplight
golden as the air.

The moon is cut in half.
The leaves of the locust, now
mustard yellow, a sophisticated color,
chastise me like an old lover would –
Your thoughts are sophistry, they say,

the truth is, Sally died today.

Sally's heart is a large heart
in the carriage of her body,
and horses rush it away.

FOR ROBERT CREELEY

when you died
I stood outside
and felt you gone
and felt you here since
you were able to say
what we long to hear one
another say, each one,
one by one,
and art, then, had meaning
not a usual one
an actual one

SELAH*
     for Denise Levertov

                         Every day, every day I hear enough
                         to fill a year of nights with wondering.

One more day of sun on snow
would have pleased you.
Your mother at ninety sighed:
'*How tired I am*
of appreciating the gift of life.'

   *

Somerville

nothing too neat, a small house
in a cul de sac, half-hidden from the street

   *

I hold out my hand to a bird with a smooth peach color,
it disappears in the headlights.

Is your spirit in the west, in personless spaces,
in grey and green, last decade of your life.

   *

Green of the streetlight
running liquid down the lane.

I turn *The Jacob's Ladder* over
but no picture of you there,
only black and granite.

Decades before my father's blindness
you wrote about looking
at the blind man on the subway: *He knows*
where he is going, it is nowhere, it is filled
with presences. He says, ' I am.'

Many the girls you mothered,
making distinctions, sitting straight,
ever the ballerina. Intuiting each line break.
Precision, earnestness –

the saints you wrote of with descriptive love.

*

smoke of noise on the small highway

tar swirls in the grey street

*

after the memorial celebration

out past a heavy church door
a large sun floods a soft sky

on the drive home
autoharp and fiddle
and a woman's clear tones

for many, you were soprano and alto

*

largesse, gap-toothed laugh –
her comeliness
dissipates, glitters, in our tiny dawn

** A Hebrew word of unknown meaning often marking the end of a verse in the
Psalms and thought to be a term indicating a pause or rest*

ANNE SEXTON ON THE COVER

Your cigarette could be a piece of chalk.
(You were telling us *This class is saving my life*.)
Bracelets handcuff you, hands raised to heaven.

Puffed up hair, full of smoke. Your eyebrows plucked,
pleading. You're smiling, shoulders bare,
yet your legs are crossed tightly, snakes coupling.

Your dress: swirls of chocolate and vanilla, mud and snow.
Fingernails, short, fingers, long,
limbs, long, desire, long, longer than
a garden party at which you are this evening's star.

Your name, plastered across your lap on the book jacket,
wraps you in a golden bow. Today in Harvard Square,
the statue of seated Sumner wore an apron of snow.
I was tired of the gender of things, you wrote.

A glass of booze next to you, nearly empty.
It's summer, you're divorced, the thick ring,
its huge stone slid to the side
on your right hand now.

But if I hadn't known you, what would I see?
A long, thin woman, hopeful, sad, poised
against rejection. Or a strong one,
politic, sure of her next move.

They want blood, you said after your last reading.
Voyeurs. I'm never going to read again, and it was true –
I immerse myself in your biography; you were
famous for your false self, I'm looking for you.

FOR GEORGI BELEV

As your words crackled then fell off,
roses made layered shadows on the black floor,
magic wand shadow of the microphone.

To the right of you, under lights,
sun and moon shadow of a round table,
water glasses and carafes upside down like diamond hourglasses.

Backdrop of a dream of mountains.

You wore a white shirt with a small collar,
pale jeans and the plainest of black shoes.
The little books from which you read
had understated covers, the color of sand.
Like mine your skin is pale, your hair dark.

In the street there were
people I'm used to who seem unlike me,
and street lights orange and lemon.
These summer nights
when I won't go inside I just keep walking –
traffic lights like planets, the crickets, wind.

Along this river
reflections – bronze and silver and palest green,
like a disco, or some intricate weaving,
like zippers, zigzags
through the water, everything fluid, metallic melt.

IMAGINING THE IMPRISONMENT OF MS. LU HSIU-LIEN

People talking in restaurants
with absorption and great seriousness
about baseball or expanding their business.
How we limit ourselves.
A trick of reading in near dark,
denying darkness beyond lamp or room.

I didn't want to imagine it.
I wanted to imagine it.

Woman or man –
one of the few times when that makes no difference.
Vulnerable as cows in their stalls,
which are all the world then.

But if the person tortured is a woman.
I know the curves of a woman.
I don't want to imagine them hurt, but I can.

What I won't imagine are the rooms,
the unchanging months.

*Ms. Lu Hsiu-Lien was arrested on December 10 (Human Rights Day)
in Kaohsuing, Taiwan, after a human rights rally that ended in rioting....She
received a Master's degree from Harvard....
She was one of two feminist writers convicted....Her publications
include 'New Feminism,' 'The Past and Future of Taiwan,' and 'The
Amendment for Legalizing Abortion.'...Reportedly, she must read
books assigned by the prison authorities and write lengthy favorable
reviews of them. She has been forbidden to use the words* peace *and* human
rights.

Just so, Muriel Rukeyser insisted,
no distinction between the political and the personal:
*...he sees the sharp fear pass
verdict upon her, pitching and frothing toward the
mechanical white walls.*

To some, love must be

unreal as sunshine in rooms
where there's no day, wind, summer.

I imagine

that some still find the stream of love in the body,
feel it flow to the prisoner in the next cell,
if there is a next cell.

Some die from what was done to them,
some are not allowed to die.

We have been more savage than not.
Often we forget that,
write,
without pressure,
believe in language –
Lu Hsiu-Lien's captors do.
For her, we write *peace* and *human rights*,
that much we are willing to do.

PARTS OF YOU
            for Claudia

Summer, the season in which everything is here.
A wet night in August keeps her up.
Her husband sleeps well,
having learned, in a ripped childhood,
read and sleep.
She looks at the room.
The cat's pink ball
gray in the dark.
Tomorrow afternoon scores of pigeons
will glide by, close to the grey street.
The next season, here soon,
a break with this flat world.
On wet nights
the wait keeps her awake.

*

This part is new.
Your mind must be turning.

Who could have guessed it?
You were a circle before,
a warm atheist.
You knew what you said and you said it.

Now you say new words, painfully,
words like anger, spirituality.

It makes you feel taller,
this intellect. It is something
you once had no use for.

Your apartment is old wood, and white.
Unexpectedly – you love a cat.
You write with hard edges,
that picture of your family's fading,
you're thinner.

*

As though she had taken a long subway ride
and finally gotten off at a silent station,
divorce.
She walks in new rooms
and her letters are addressed to me.
I go to sleep.
Sleep.
A strange word, dark, and thin.
Everything I know is sleep.
Around her heart, black.
Around her white room, white.

A WOMAN ON *THE NEWS HOUR*

She leans forward, her arms on the desk.
She looks like Mick Jagger.
She wears a thick silver necklace.
Black sheen is her hair.
Her earrings are big black dots.
When she smiles her nose turns down.
She wears a black-and-white checked jacket.
She's thin, and short.
She's always going to fit in.
She's always a little different.
She is herself, whoever she is.
An empty water glass is half visible in front of her.
Her face is sinking.

LOBBY OF A NEW YORK RESIDENTIAL HOTEL

They're wearing bandanas and black eye make-up, and they've pinned up their hair. They're probably in their sixties:

She used to go out with that little faggot man.
Never. She never did. He wanted to go out with her, but she had all the men she needed. He was on dope, also, and she was so against dope you have no idea.
He was on dope? I'm very surprised. I'm very surprised. You know when I first moved in here I was very naive.
But you're not now.
I'm not now but I was very naive at one time.
Jane just called to say that she's not coming down after all.
I knew that, I knew that already before she called you.

A very old, very drunk man goes over to the magazine stand and says, I'd like to buy some cocaine.
We're all out of cocaine.
Then give me the number of the man, you know, the head of the Mafia, and I'll call him and get it from him.
I can't give you that number. It's a secret.
I can understand that. I'll tell you what. I'll give you the number and you can call him.

I'm all out of food. I have to eat tonight.
I had a Swiss cheese sandwich last night for dinner but I can't be expected to go shopping for food every night.
If I had to take care of somebody else I couldn't afford to feed him.
Do you eat lobster?
Sure. It's good. It's not filling, though.
You know what my daughter used to eat with lobster?
Steak?
How'd you know? Steak that thick, oh, boy. Food isn't so expensive out there. Whenever I went to see them, my son-in-law brought us to the most expensive restaurants. They treated him like he was the President of the United States. They have maitre d's out there. They treated me like I was a celebrity.
I know. I've been out there.
So I don't have to tell you.

I went down south for several months once. Worst thing I ever did. I would never give up my apartment again.
I did that, too.
You just went there to visit. I went there to live.
I was there two months.
I was there two days and came back. All my furniture was gone and everything.

PROFILE OF A POTATO HEAD
after a painting by Philip Guston

Here's a cup I use as a pencil holder.

Cigarette butts like bricks of old cake fill the plate.

The one I'm smoking feels like a block of wood, smoldering.

I lie on my back on a plank, wrapped in swaddling clothes, mummified.

You can see the mammoth white of one eye.

I dreamt that I was going to die, woke up before I found out what happened.

No one's dropped in for a week.

He's painted my hair coral.
Everything's got coral stuck on it.

My head's hard.
Everything in my room is hard.

Even my shoes are stiff, lined up; the nails stick out the bottoms.
I'm sore I'm so stiff.

My heart's chipped, like a mug or an Egyptian bust.

CONCERT AT THE GARDNER MUSEUM

The guard looks up and sees an angel with a vest of gold sequins and a silver spear. He begins the applause for the entering musicians. The pianists play the duet hunched over and sloppily, but when the ensemble begins the Ravel he sees their mouths open in concentration, he hears a composer leaving a melody. The violinist leans sideways and back, as though the music were a circle in which he could rest. The cellist is the woman who blushed when I saw her putting on make-up in the bathroom. Her nose is straight, her lips thin, and the neck of the cello curves into a chestnut ear that curls beside her small and pearly one.

A bearded blond man sits down next to me. He's wearing a brown leather jacket; he leans forward, in control and alone. He could be at a party, doing coke, but he turns to me and asks, *Have they played one piece or two? Two.* This music is order and dream. After the applause, we all return to what we cannot share. The music, chestnut, silver, and maroon, has faded into the tapestry of the room. The silver-haired guard, his forehead shining, checks the exits.

THE OLD HIGH WAY OF LOVE

Mirage of gentle colors,
that distant, aesthetic way of love.

In dreams you bent away from me.

You burned hot and cold simultaneously,
your thoughts like dry ice, smoky.
I watched the visible waves of you,
wheat-color curls at the sides of your neck.

I watched you sleep until the sun,
bleak and raw, smeared the horizon.

Raindrops drying on meadow grass in morning.

CLARK PARK

The trolleys fence us in
in the park where we most often sit
separately. When we talk
it's often disappointing.

I look across at my house
where I don't want
to go. I imagine
myself sitting inside.

I feel
threatened, anxious,
lonely, though
at times I'm peaceful.

Six trees in a row.
Their trunks are solid,
just enough space between them.

I know if you touched me
I could relax.
I went looking for you, angry
at myself for that.

COURTYARD CONCERT

Music like wind.
The flutist teases out from his silver flute
the song of a young girl he's loved.
Patient cello, it's had its turn for now.
The green drums gleam; the chimes
a Marchese's necklace.
Grey curtains of the stage
ruffles in the breezes.

What will I tell you?
City, wood and stone.
Silent sculptures of muscular men.
I'll write you a letter and tell you about tonight,
though if I feel you through my body
am I away from you?

There's a frieze of a donkey on a cornerstone.
A cat trots by. You have a cat. What am I?
Palazzo Pitti, the deepening sky?
The star or two
that doesn't need a bird to fly to it,
the chimes, the boy
softly striking the cymbals?
Keeping time, then breaking it?
You tell me a little, a little lie.
A rush of keyboard, ocean foam bubbles by.

STEPS

You put a towel over the lampshade and climb on me, slowly
play with the zipper of my jeans.

We go downstairs and you fry me a baloney sandwich,
drink my whiskey.

Olive-skinned, wiry, your hair wild
black and kinky. I watch you make love to me.
*
The way you inhale the smoke of a cigarette.
You kiss the back of my neck for a long time.
I pull your hair.
Until dawn – the stars,
the umbrella, the fireplace –
everything the same as you are.
*
I dreamt I tied you to a tree. You snapped it in half and walked away.
*
Long after you left I lay on the sofa bed.
*
We do everything in your studio.
Maroon velveteen sofa.
Candles in glasses.
Wine from styrofoam cups.
Herb tea, dry, crinkles in a purple and yellow box.
You're purple and yellow.
*
I dreamt a green snake climbed through my stomach, its head entered my
throat.

What if your eyes seem sometimes soft?
They go from kindness to blackness in a flash.
What if your cheekbones are craggy?
The next day you were gone.
*
I looked at the drapery, measured it
with my stick of charcoal. I drew the top,
the folds at the bottom, connected them,

stepped back, squinted, erased with my finger
places where the shading was too dark.

I think about first impressions, outlines, nuances.
*
Developing allergies late in life is neurotic,
you say, the other night. I get mad.
Why get mad? you ask. *Are you ashamed of your neuroses?*

... Your black eyes and black curls
and your prancing around my bedroom
in my red and gold Chinese jacket –
but I have nightmares after I'm with you.
*
Just from being around you, I dance in my livingroom,
go riding in my car very late.
*
In your eyes I saw the steps of a temple
I wanted to climb.
First leaves of spring, leaves of fall, greenish brown.
I saw salmon swim, flickers of kindness.

When you became wooden what I had seen
in your eyes died. Even in my dream
you turned yourself into a work of art.
I saw a puppet, wooden on one side,
painted with black and brown stripes,
eyes wide and dyed.

When I woke up, at dawn,
the round orange sun at the window,
it was the day for my dog to die.

And I was peaceful. But when I called you to say,
please come over,
you refused.
So I created an animal of snow.
*
I watch you as you use words, make sentences just to make them,
break them, make rejection into metaphor, come
over, and I can't tell if you're asking to leave or to stay.
Lately we make love during the day and at night you go away
to make charcoal drawings of the severed heads of men.

58

*

You cross your skinny legs, your wrists are princely.
I yell, I throw a blanket at you, you catch it,
you roll it up, you put it away, and put your hands on my legs
and we're off again. I climb on top of you and you say,

That is you and I'm in Oxon Hill again with a gang of kids,
they're breaking a window and running away, Irish Catholic,
like you, I use my mouth the way I like.
I pour beer on you, too.
*

I find a note in my bedroom: *To Ruby,*
I owe you one (1) orgasm. Tony.
*

when the sun makes a strobe light
of trees I drive by, at a certain speed –
my mind goes blank
*

I transcribed an interview
with Philip Guston years ago,
you find it now and read it aloud to me.

You extorted pocket change
from the intellectual kids in your high school,
you told me.
*

Maple trees – paint brushes, spears –
fill the air with rain.
Summer's wet,
and you're not even here yet.

I stay in,
something medieval in my dreams.
*

Your eyes are my mother's dark eyes,
your eyes are my first love's, cold blue,
your eyes are my ex-husband's, hieroglyphs.
*

black strokes across my body
like Egon Schiele sketches

Aztec cheekbones,
your face a triangle,

a ram's head

even your handwriting
well proportioned
*

for a time you paint with tar
but you're tidy in the way
you get away from every place
*

I brought roses to your friends.
They were kinder to me than they were to you,
but it took me a while to notice.

After dinner you said,
I haven't seen the studio for a year,
let's go back there.
We sat on the steps in the hall.
All I could think of
was how to keep you interested
so I could watch the lines of your face a little longer.
I didn't notice that sentence by sentence you were dismembering my life.
You went back to Chicago without calling.
*

I'm a middle-aged woman, I fell in love.
It's a year later, you call out of the blue
and say, *Why don't you come to Chicago?*

SORRY

Sorry, I was shut down.
Sorry, I was doing my work.
Sorry, well, actually, I don't give a shit.
Sorry, I needed to get my life together.
Sorry, I'm a vacuum.
Sorry, I don't feel anything.
Sorry, just because I'm in love with you
doesn't mean I'm going to have a relationship with you.
Sorry, I needed to watch this TV show.
It's just that I'm too unhappy to help you.
I was drunk.
I was stoned.
Sorry, I was attracted to you and couldn't help myself.

ROSE

one I loved has virtually no response when I tell him something
sad, freeing me to exist in a world in which
the specifics of life are a higher moral calling
happy and high am I to be there then

– red rose in the back of the mind

Bonnard red

AN EDGE OF GOLD

Light
surrounded the first few men
I loved, as though
their bodies were denser molecules of light,
light that scattered
an edge of gold.

Just last night,
you, the plain one,
plain since you see me,
turned around,
your mouth relaxed,
and gold was around you,

I'm afraid of so much desire –
desire makes distinctions –
gold's in everything,
I'm in love with just you.

At the moment of death
is there a letting go
or is the desire so great
for everything.

MARRIAGE

Nine years ago we found each other, foggy, in a clear world.
I couldn't talk to you at first but I wanted you,
you were like me, and my opposite, too.

After lunches in which we tried to discuss history,
at last an evening with you.
I shook until you showed me pictures of everyone you knew.
When you started to turn away at the door I couldn't let you go,
the pretty boy who argued,
gestures sweet as spring air.
What am I going to do with you? I said,
and when I kissed you the air got soft.

For years neither of us knew how to be married,
both of us were powerless,
the other could take everything away
with one false syllable,
so we couldn't afford to give in –
you are the only person who has seen most of my life.

After you came back from your walk through Quebec City
to our relatively grand hotel,
we celebrated your 30th birthday with breakfast in our carpeted room.
Those mocha pastries with the sizzling sparklers reminded me of us,
and I pushed you to say
it was the happiest, the best birthday you'd ever had.

You kept after me to row better last week
although in the past you had complimented me
on my ability to row smoothly,
a trait which seemed to surprise you.
I tried as hard as I could to row well
then told you to leave me alone.
At nearly the end of the trip we traded paddles.
I got the wooden one.
This plastic paddle's a piece of shit, you said.
No wonder you couldn't row.
Why didn't you say something?

Yesterday we picked raspberries in Concord.
I should say *I* picked raspberries
while you talked to a high school exchange student from Bologna
and I remembered the arboretum in Montréal
where we'd seen a tree with orange berries.
Isn't that spectacular? you'd said.
I've never seen anything like it.
And I'd said, *Those berries are all over Massachusetts.*
There's a whole bunch of them down the street from our apartment.
Years ago I would've said that condescendingly,
but that time I said it laughingly, though still hoping to perfect.
Today I walked along the Charles and there was one of those trees.
Today it had orange leaves, so the berries didn't stand out so glaringly,
as the difference between you and me is one of shape, not color.

We call each other Cooks and Cranston, Quiddity,
the names change, I forget who's who,
a long line of love, the links forgotten.

An hour ago a startled squirrel looked down at me
and I looked up at it and talked in the way I talk to animals,
a way you think is eccentric (but you're glad I wanted a dog),
and the squirrel looked like you –
I thought it would turn into a rat if cornered,
a dove if soothed,
and its grey-brown body could hardly contain
the streaming movement in the bright world of fall,
your favorite season, mid-October leaves screaming
in the sky. On the ground,
two maple leaves, one yellow, one green and grey,
intertwined, and I hoped
that we would die together, you, the unknowable side
of the world, a man, and I.

LOVE

New ceilings, new views.
This afternoon you came home early,
and by 3:30 we were naked and smiling.
We remembered that we live together until death
and that things float away as we move through seasons.
How many things we have accumulated in these years,
how they have kept us busy, and dulled.
Good-bye, old house, we love you as we leave.
We have lived here long enough.

GRASSES

We rode the hills on horseback,
hills curved like horses,
long grass, black earth giving way.

Rode on back of a bumpy haycart
to Pot o' Gold – where, half the night,
in fog, you fished.

It's a rickety bus we took
up the stunted western coast.

Deep green of the sward,
the poor towns of Ireland,
men so saltily beautiful.

*

Once I slept in a ditch in South Dakota,
startled by trucks that went whizzing by.
Across the highway, all lit up, a truck stop.
All lit up, like you.
                    In the morning
I was walking in a ten-house town,
the grass bluish,
and a horse, free to roam, clomped
up to me, as I watched the town
waking.

FEBRUARY

The snow blows close to me,
closer than anyone would dare to come.
A music that covers me.
A man turns, I touch his face, we're
spinning, helpless again
in the white meadow.

THEY WERE

They were gliding down the river,
I remember.
He leaned toward the turquoise water,
would not tell her what he wanted.
She tried hard to read the paper,
I remember,
she was tired,
couldn't read the Sunday paper,
couldn't smile or reach his hand.

Worried, he would tip the boat a little,
he would tip it without warning.
Only she fell in, remember,
freezing water, creatures under.
Caught in seaweed, I remember.
She was grateful when he saved her.
She was shaking,
he felt better,
I remember.

THE BOY

is a cold dream.
like the sea.
on the surface scary, empty.

small waves, thousands,
clambering over one another:
this is business.

once in a while, under.
his creatures,
warm currents.

SEPARATION

Like lines in ink on a thin piece of paper
tossed to the sea, so soon
the story of our marriage dissolves.

Yesterday I swam in the ocean.
It was the first thing in months that felt like you,
covering my shoulders. I burst out laughing.
It hit me in the stomach, knocked me down.
At moments the slow sound of it
caught my attention, I breathed heavily.

Some time recently I stopped looking for you
at every turn, in every silver car.
Now I sit on rocks that turn molten
in the sunset, and watch other fishermen
as a hundred times I watched you fish.

I know,
if you and I were like the sea and me,
wordless and touching, if you and I
could walk along holding hands, speechless,
the way the ocean does not speak...
            There's a seagull, yelling its need at me.

I felt your love like a ribbon,
a nearly white silken ribbon –
each day you came home after me,
tied it 'round me.

MOTION SICKNESS: PRE-OCCUPATION

Xeroxing and a doughnut,
then, outdoors, a rush of pigeons.
*

All the world's a stage
I'm going through.
*

Though it's sunny
the car in front of me squirts
windshield wiper fluid that
swirls back and sticks to my hair.
*

It's scary, said Kathy –
who proofreads ancient Greek –
*You're driving to work
and suddenly you're there
and you don't know how you got there.*
*

I dreamt you had a girlfriend
who made candy wrappers for a living.
Random cortical movement, narrative added?
*

Mayakovsky:
*like a slave
I am rocking my body with madness.*
*

Her silhouette at the play,
simple as a doll's.
*

The woman next door listening
to *The Moonlight Sonata* and, simultaneously, a soap opera.
*

First thing in the morning –
an orange cat with a ripped seagull in its mouth,
running through my rock garden.
*

I felt like a sack of sugar, leaking. Your girlfriend
looked like a cross
between Barbara and George Bush.
*

I didn't write stories,
because they took too much of the energy
I needed to think about you.
*

I'm prone.
*

There's that feeling of after-summer-rain
again.

FIX

My moon-stained mind won't fix
on last night's lemon and blue-clay sky
since in the night you came by.

I dreamt I had swum out
to the middle of the grey, grey sea,
you'd landed a plane there
and were waiting for me
but refused after all to take me home –
so I swam
half way back –
or did I come to a shore
where others were.

ESCALATOR

Yesterday I rode down a thin escalator
and last night falling asleep
I saw myself as a girl, swinging
on a long rope close to the bottom of a hill.
From the steepest of hills,
I wondered if I could get down to her again.
I woke tired.

This morning I'll go to the divorce hearing.
I looked up "husband" in the dictionary.
It comes from "living in the house."
I looked up "wife."
Wife meant woman, woman was wife.
I looked up marriage.
It comes from *maritus*, husband,
from whom I go
to find how a woman can live beyond wife.

THE DAY OF OUR DIVORCE HEARING

you treated me to lunch, a spaghetti place.
We had never been so kind to each other.
When you said *I'm still a slob* we laughed.
After lunch we stood in the parking lot.
You said, *You have the last word*
but I said, *No, I'm tired of being
the one who sums things up.
You get the last word.*
But you couldn't think of one.
So off you went to our silver car,
I to our red one.
It's three years later.
And even that's just a story now.
Lately I don't feel as if I lived with you.
But I remember our kindness that day,
when it no longer mattered.

DISSOLUTION

The way the shapes on the screen saver fly and collapse and dissolve and close and open and disappear reminds me of you, or should I say that you were a metaphor for all of those kinds of shapes taking place in me, which is why I loved you for so long, and still do. When I came home tonight I cried as I often do after seeing people I knew when we were married. I love you as much as I ever did, which is as much as a wife ever loved a husband, as I said and you agreed on the day of our divorce. Tell the truth, says a friend, but what is there to tell? Thunderclap, icicles, terror, blue.

EARLY WINTER

        I close my eyes like Betty Boop –
lashes like spiders –
fringed curtain
so I can stay in my house.
I feel my eyes underneath,
my mind.   And when I open my eyes
it's still dark,
lavender and purple
at the bottom of the sky.
Time to get up.
We're divorced.

HE CALLED AND ALL*

he called and all
I could give him was some kind of
melancholy justice
an avenue at best
was I looking mainly for pleasure
depriving myself of pleasure
understanding a kind of resolution
of grief
under the pleasure at evening's end
the bitter dark
and yet again
I persisted
till I saw raindrops of late fall
and smiled since life
is surrounded with life
the trees surround the village
what was coming next
took most of a lifetime

*after Lee Hyla's setting of John Ashbery's "At North Farm"